How To Start An Online Business:

Create A Business Around Your Biggest Passion, Even If You Are Starting From Scratch

Table Of Contents

Introduction

I want to thank you and congratulate you for downloading the book How To Start An Online Business: Create A Business Around Your Biggest Passion, Even If You Are Starting From Scratch

This book contains proven steps and strategies on how to become a truly successful founder, owner, and operator of an online business. You'll learn to create a business around your biggest passion, share your products and services with others, and create a powerful spiral of upwards success and abundance.

Here's an inescapable fact: you will need specific skills and competencies to succeed at online business. Although you already have much of the basic knowledge simply by virtue of being an empathic human being, there are specific tips and tricks that you can only learn through careful study. This book has them all but delivers these core competencies and skills in the context of tapping into your innate business-mindedness and capacity to create high-quality products and services that you can then use to bring value to the lives of others.

If you do not develop your basic Internet marketing and business skills, however, you might not succeed at realizing your dream, creating a successful online business around your biggest passion, and ultimately sharing your gifts with the world.

It's time for you to become an amazing online business owner and operator. The time is now for you to share your gifts with the world, and to profit in the process.

Chapter 1: What's Your Real Passion?

People start their online businesses for all kinds of reasons. Many want the freedom to earn a comfortable living from anywhere in the world, or to create multiple passive streams of income without relying on workers or a physical business location. Still others prefer the creative freedom available through customized online media, digital products, and the user experience.

Although many online entrepreneurs accomplish their initial financial, creative, and personal goals, those who stay in the game and truly appreciate the fruits of their labors have one thing in common: they've constructed their online businesses on the solid foundation of their true passions.

Yes, it may seem paradoxical at first. Many people choose a career in business over, say, the arts for example, because they want to achieve financial stability. However, if you take a look around, all of the game changers in the business world built their empires around their passions. In this growth-oriented business climate, it's important to stand out among the competition, and one of the best ways to do that is by offering a product, service, or experience to the marketplace that improves people's lives or speaks to their authentic selves, and the best way to do that is to follow your path of authenticity and actualization, and the best way to do that is to invest fully in your real passion.

So, what is your real passion? Welcome to yet another paradox. It's an inherently difficult question to answer due to the seemingly infinite variety of passions available to us in this fast-paced, complex world. This may be the reason so many people never get around to starting their businesses. There are too many options.

To that end, the first step of your journey to online business success is to come up with an answer to the above question. Although the prospect of starting one's own online business can seem daunting from afar, and can remain daunting to those who approach the endeavor solely to earn money, once you've identified your real passion the rest will unfold with ease. And don't worry! You're not alone in this search for your real passion. The rest of this chapter includes a practical exercise you can use to find your real passion.

Exercise: Finding Your Real Passion

What you'll need:

You'll want something to write with. A computer with a word processor will work just as well as a few sheets of blank paper and a pen or pencil.

Step 1: Cluster Brainstorming

Cluster Brainstorming is a technique used in a variety of settings to assist people in fostering insight. It has applications in personal journaling for self-growth, and many creative professionals use the technique to rule out bad ideas and identify viable projects.

We'll begin with this exercise to tap into your intuitive faculties. Why don't we keep it logical? Well, human beings are complex creatures. We're both rational and creative. Most people know that success in business requires pragmatism and careful forethought. However, what works to keep a mature business afloat in a competitive marketplace might not necessarily work during the initial conceptual stages. In spite of our best intentions, we can do harm to the longevity of our business if we repress our creative, intuitive process during these fruitful and tender beginning stages.

Cluster Brainstorming is particularly helpful in bypassing the rational mind. With this technique, you'll be able to get all your ideas out, see how they fit together and get an intuition for which ideas are genuinely meaningful to you.

To do Cluster Brainstorming, simply pull out a blank piece of paper and write, in the center of the page, the following question: What's my real passion? Next, draw around it. From here, simply write your associations on the page. These may be individual words, sentences, sentence fragments, or anything else that seems appropriate to you. As you write these associations, go ahead and circle them as you did the initial question. Draw lines connecting the associations as you go, so that you can track your intuitive process as it unfolds.

Don't worry about doing this correctly. There is no right or wrong way to do it once you've got the basic procedure of writing and connecting associations. The most important thing is that you trust your intuition.

Give yourself about ten or fifteen minutes to do this exercise. You don't want to spend all day with it, but you also don't want to stop before you've let yourself indulge in the creative process. Likewise, there is no need to cover the entire page, nor is there any particular urgency to get all of your ideas onto the page. Rather, allow for pauses in writing as they come, and list your associations with ease.

When you're done, briefly pause and take a look at your web of associations. Circle those that stood out to you as particularly relevant or true.

Step 2: Exploratory Writing

This step is designed to synthesize and bring coherence to your map of associations. Turn the page over and, at the top, write: What's my real passion? See if you can write continually in response to this question without stopping for a good five minutes.

Once you've done that, stop, read it over, and then see if you can complete the following statements, limiting your responses to one or two sentences, no more than three. The purpose of this part of the exercise is to hone your real passion.

My real passion is…

My real passion is not…

I thought my real passion was…

But then I realized…

When I was a child, my real passion was…

When I was an adolescent, my real passion was…

I know that my real passion is [blank] because…

I have known that [blank] is my real passion for [blank] years.

I first realized that [blank] was my real passion when…

Now, give yourself another five minutes and, once more, write continuously without censoring yourself in response to the following question: What's my real passion?

By now, you likely have a good sense of what your real passion is. However, it's perfectly normal to not know quite yet. If you need more time, continue to try this two-step exercise until you gain a solid idea of what your true passion is.

If, after some time, you are still unsure of what your real passion is, consider making an appointment with a career coach. Career coaches are experts at helping you identify what you love, and have some tests and other tools and measures at their disposal. Even the greatest of the greats have turned to career coaches in times of need. These professionals are highly valuable to entrepreneurs, and an appointment is certainly worth your time and money.

Speaking of money, by now you might be wondering how to take your real passion and turn it into a profitable business. In the next chapter, you'll learn to link your passion to the needs, desires, and interests of potential customers, clients, and patrons of your online business. This is an exciting time. You are about to begin a journey to self-fulfillment and financial security.

Chapter 2: Find The Most Profitable Niche In 7 Simple Steps

Welcome to one of the biggest secrets in the online business world: Internet entrepreneurship is both an art and science. It is an art in that creating a business, forecasting its impact on culture, and offering products that are of true value to customers are inherently creative acts. On the other hand, forecasting and maintaining the viability of the business is a little more pragmatic. This secret is most clearly illustrated in the process of selecting a profitable niche market.

Often, this process is described as if it were about identifying those segments of the Internet in which people spend the most money or click on the most advertisements. Although there is a small amount of truth to this description, it misses one very significant factor. The extent to which a niche is considered "profitable" has to do both with the above factors and the extent to which you as the business owner are prepared to ensure the viability of your product. Hence the importance of identifying your real passion and constructing your business on something that will drive you to succeed.

The truth is that, in most cases, the extent to which a niche is popular depends on a marketer's ability to survey the territory, alert people to a given product, and, with the assistance of the business owner, ensure that the product is of high quality according to those who purchase it. One note is that in the world of online business, the business owner and the marketer are often the same people. To that end, it's typically up to you to both create and market your product. The good new is, if your product is something you're truly passionate about, there is a good chance you already have a sense of how and to whom you can successfully market your product.

In the steps that follow, you'll learn how to identify market niches specific to your product, how to estimate their general likelihood of yielding profit, and finally how to identify and capitalize upon what exactly makes those niches profitable in the first place. Who knows? At the end of these seven steps, you might find yourself well on your way to becoming one of the major players in your market.

Step 1: Get Specific

One of the most fundamental aspects of identifying a profitable niche is the process of getting specific. Do you remember the exercises from the previous chapter? You might have come up with one answer in response to the question of your real passion. Or, if you're like most people, you narrowed down a few things you're deeply passionate about. If you still have them, pull out your writings from the previous chapter.

Take a look both at your web of associations and your exploratory writings. Choose a couple or a few topics that you might like to construct a business around. Now, make a column on the left-hand side of a blank sheet of paper. In that column, go ahead and list these couple or few topics, with plenty of space between them.

Now, think about more specific subcategories of these topics. As you think of specific subcategories, go ahead and write them to the right of each of the main topics. From there, continue to jot down subcategories of the subcategories, and so on.

Here's an example. Say you were passionate about nutrition. You might end up writing a string of subcategories like the following:

Nutrition – Vegetarian Nutrition – Vegetarian nutrition on the go – Nutritious Vegetarian recipes for travelers on the go.

Eventually, you might consider settling on the niche market of nutritious vegetarian recipes for travelers on the go.

Step 2: Google Trends

Once you've got a few possible niche markets, it's time to investigate their popularity. Go ahead and head over to **www.google.com/trends/** to get a sense of how popular your niches are. With Google Trends, you can see how popular a topic is, and whether or not its popularity is waning. Best practice is to avoid those topics that might be waning in popularity. The best niches either rapidly increasing in popularity, or consistently popular over time. Of course, if it's something you're deeply passionate about, you can always consider investing your time and, possibly, money in a niche that is waning in popularity. Who knows? Your business might spark a revival in a given area of interest.

Step 3: Survey The Territory

Once you've established that a niche is viable given the quantitative data in Google Trends, go ahead and gather some qualitative data on your terms. Take a look at what people are saying about your niche on forums. Look at what other businesses in your niche area are doing to provide quality products to interested customers. Check out blogs and, if applicable, magazines and trade publications. See if there are any informational products available for purchase.

The purpose of this step is two-fold: On one hand, you want to see what's out there. As you search, you should be thinking about what kind of product and information you'd like to provide to customers. This is the perfect time to get inspired. Take tips from those who have already entered the market and think about how you might offer something unique.

On the other hand, if you determine that others are indeed earning a profit in a given niche, you should ask yourself if you have a product that will be valuable amidst the competition. Keep in mind that it's easier than one might think to break into a given market. However, with that in mind, if you feel overwhelmed by the potential competition in a given niche, or if it feels too far outside of your comfort zone, move on to another that suits you better. At this stage, you want to consider both the profit inherent in a given niche and your unique ability to earn a profit in said niche.

Step 4: Make A Categorical Distinction

Niche markets exist for a few reasons. As a businessperson, you'll want to be parsimonious in the reason you attribute to the existence of a given niche market. To that end, of the following reasons, see if you can select one, and only one, reason to account for the existence of the niche market(s) you've identified and investigated so far.

People might be drawn to a niche market:

1. In search of the answer to a problem.

2. Because the topic is interesting.

3. Because the topic is personally meaningful.

4. In search of resources that might assist one in excelling in one's profession.

5. In search of experiences, that might contribute to personal growth.

6. Because it is entertaining.

Step 5: Identify Your Gift

Take a moment to review what conclusions you've come to so far as you've moved through these steps. Now, at this time, take another moment to jot down a few ideas you have about the kind of online business you want to create. Ask yourself the following questions:

What kind of informational product might I provide?

What will the content and structure of my written materials be like?

Who might read them?

What might my reader gain from my product and my business?

Don't spend too much time on these questions as we'll go into much greater detail about them in subsequent chapters. For now, concentrate on getting a rough sketch of the value you might be able to offer to patrons of a given niche via your business. When you're ready, spend about five minutes journaling in response to the following question: What is my gift?

When you're done, recall some of the qualitative data you gathered in the third step. Can you see your product fitting in, or standing out? What might patrons of your selected niche have to say about your online business? What would you like them to say about it?

Step 6: Identify Your Angle

This is the time to flush briefly what you envision the contribution of your business to be. It helps to think of each niche as a subculture within a larger culture. A niche has its ecosystem, its rules, and norms. Ask yourself the following questions, and jot down any thoughts that seem noteworthy to you.

1. How can I make a valuable contribution to the content that defines this niche?

2. Is my content new, or is it a new twist on something that's been around for a while?

3. Who in this niche will benefit from my online business?

4. How will I stand out from others in this niche?

If you can come up with a somewhat concrete sense of how you will make a positive, yet unique contribution to the already existing niche community that you intend to assimilate into via your online business, then there is a good chance you've found a niche that is both objectively profitable and subjectively profitable for you in light of your interests and passion.

Step 7: Make A List

There is a final test. Can you make a list of about 20 blog post title unique to your given niche? If you can, and if you believe members of the niche population would be interested in reading those blog posts, then there's a good chance the product or service you have to offer would yield a profit if marketed to that particular niche. At this point, it is likely that you've identified a profitable niche. Congratulations! You're ready to assemble your online business.

Chapter 3: Search An Unsolved Problem In Your Niche

The best way to find profit in a given niche is to identify a way in which you can be of service to the population of that niche. The best way to find out how to be of service is to get to know said population. Do you remember the qualitative data you gathered in the third step of the previous chapter? Well, in this chapter, you'll learn to deepen that process to identify the most profitable aspects of an already profitable niche. To be clear, unsolved problems are the goldmines of a given niche.

To get started, return to the task of visiting forums, blogs, websites, and business pages specific to your niche. Don't forget to check out YouTube videos and other media. See if there's a sub-Reddit dedicated to your preferred niche. Don't forget to read the comments in blogs and on video tube sites specific to your niche.

For now, you want to get a very thorough understanding of who occupies your niche. Eventually, you should be able to answer the following questions:

1. What brings people to this niche market?

2. Why do people stay once they've arrived?

3. How has participation in this niche market improved the lives of those who populate it?

4. Have people expressed a lack of any particular information product or service? If so, what is this lack?

5. Have people expressed any disappointments? If so, what are they?

6. Have people expressed a desire for any particular product or service? If so, what product or service?

7. As you continue to immerse yourself in this niche subculture, do you find that some product or service is missing? If so, what is it?

Once you've got a good sense of answers to the above questions, it's time to test them out in the community. Go ahead and join some of the forums that are popular in your niche's community. State your hypotheses that certain products and services are missing, and see how people respond. If members of the niche community agree, there's a good chance you have an accurate sense of an unsolved problem in your selected niche. If people disagree, however, it could indicate that you are somewhat out of touch with the needs and desires of this niche. If this is the case, continue to investigate and test your hypotheses in the community.

You might also attempt to get in touch with the major players of your niche for feedback on your hypotheses about unsolved problems specific to the niche. These so-called "major players" might be active forum members, or they may be other online business owners. Either way, this activity presents both an opportunity to solicit candid feedback on the extent to which you are attuned to the wants and needs of the community and an opportunity to forge alliances with key members of the community. In turn, these community members may be more likely to assist you in promoting your product or service and integrating it into the niche community. Furthermore, they may be grateful to you for your interest in the needs and desires of the community and your determination to improve it.

Finding an unsolved problem in your niche is a specific skill that many business owners, unfortunately, don't have. It's the skill that will set you apart from most of your competition. That is the true value of branching into specific niches. And the best part is, once you identify a niche and begin to market in that particular sector, you have a better chance of creating highly personalized informational products and services that will add massive value to the lives of those prospective customers. Furthermore, with the right skills and competencies, it's easier to establish yourself as an expert in a given niche, and thus easier to connect with the major players not only in your niche but of tertiary and complementary niches as well.

Chapter 4: Define Your Customer Avatar

At this point, you should have a pretty good sense of who occupies a given niche market. From there, you should take some time to consider who, within the niche, would be most likely to consume your products and services. Just as you identified a niche within the larger culture to couch your products and services, now you should consider yet a more specific population within the niche. This population should be so specific that it can more or less be summed up with a single "customer avatar". The following exercise should assist you in coming up with this ideal, generalized customer. It is a writing exercise, so you'll need writing materials. A computer will work just as well as a paper and pencil or pen.

Exercise: Customer Character Sketch

Artists, writers, storytellers, and, perhaps most notably, playwrights and actors use facets of the following technique to get to know their characters better. Likewise, you'll be taking your qualitative data and analysis of it to model the ideal use of your products and services. To be clear, the ideal use of your business starts with the user of your business, the customer, and so you begin with a clear sense of who exactly it is that might benefit from your products and services.

As you go through the following questions, see if you can write for between two and five minutes without pausing. Don't try to censor yourself. You want to use your associations, which have been tempered by both your extensive study of the culture of the niche, and by your participation in this culture through forums, blogs, and other means. To that end, you might find that you identify, to some extent, with the customer avatar that you create.

1. What does the customer look like?

2. What is a typical day for your customer?

3. How old is your customer?

4. What is the gender of your customer?

5. What are your customer's hopes and dreams?

6. What are your customer's fears, worries, and concerns?

7. What was your customer's experience in school?

8. What kind of clothes does your customer wear?

9. What kind of food does your customer eat?

10. What is your customer's relationship with money? How likely is he to spend it, as opposed to saving it?

11. What might motivate your customer to buy a product?

12. If your customer were faced with multiple brands of the same product, what factor would determine which brand your customer would ultimately select? Would it be, for instance, matter or price, quality, or popularity?

13. What would your customer do with one million dollars?

14. What would your customer do with one hundred dollars?

15. Is your customer an introvert or extrovert?

16. Does your customer prefer Mac or PC?

17. What kind of phone does your customer use?

18. How likely is your customer to read a novel? A magazine? A newspaper? An advertisement?

19. Does your customer prefer longer or shorter written material?

20. Does your customer prefer written material or videos?

21. How much time does your customer spend online?

22. How much time does your customer spend at work?

23. How much time does your customer spend thinking about work?

24. Return to the final step in the second chapter. How interested might your customer be in the items on the list of blog posts you generated?

Creating the customer avatar is a somewhat lengthy process. It takes time and patience and is best reserved for a couple of days given all of the writing and thinking involved. The above list is by no means an exhaustive set of questions; it is only the basic and most essential. With this list, you should be able to create a very accurate customer avatar, but if you really want to ensure success in your marketing and outreach strategies, as well as in the extent to which the patrons of your online business value your products, it is advised that you continue to generate questions and spend some time writing unabashedly in response so that you can bring your associations and ideas into your awareness.

As you continue to fill out the list, additional questions should be guided by the idiosyncratic data you gathered during your qualitative study of the niche, and also questions that are specific to the product or service you intend to sell via your online business.

Once your customer avatar is complete and filled in by your responses to the above questions, go back once more to the niche community, visiting the forums, blogs, and so on, and see if you can find members of the community who are similar to your customer avatar. If you can, that's a sign of success! If not, see if you can find out why. It may be that you simply haven't asked yourself enough orienting questions, at which point you can form a hypothesis about what information you might be missing in your ability to form a general and representative customer avatar. Then you can return to the exercise, gather the information, rewrite your customer avatar, and continue to check it against the niche population for similarity until you find that you've created a customer avatar that truly and accurately matches some aspect of the niche community to which you hope to market your products and services.

When your customer avatar is filled out, you're ready for the next chapter. From here on out, you'll be focusing on content and marketing strategies to best matching your customer avatar with your wonderful and highly useful products and services. To that end, although you might like to skim ahead and get a better sense of the overall direction of this process, it is best to refrain from investing your time in the activities described in the subsequent chapters until you have created a customer avatar that is accurately representative of some segment of your niche population.

Chapter 5: How To Maximize Your Information Product Profits: Entry Level, Core, And Upsell

Online businesses sell information products. In the model presented in this book, information products are the most likely to be profitable, considering how much time you are encouraged to invest in getting to know the niche to which you wish to market. Furthermore, this book is written in such a way that the information products should become more coherent to you as you continue through the earlier chapters. So far, you have been encouraged to consider and develop a vague idea of the kind of product you'd like to sell in relation and in tandem to your learning about who occupies the niche. Therefore, you are uniquely suited to create, market, sell, and profit from a very high-quality information product that is specifically suited to the needs of the niche. In the next chapter, you'll go through the steps of actually creating an information product. First, however, it's important to learn how to market your information product.

There is a direct relationship between the kinds of information products you sell and the kinds of information products you write. Put another way, when it comes to producing information products both to satisfy your passion for a subject and to profit from the time you've invested in the business that you constructed around your passion, you want to make sure you're earning a comfortable income as well as enjoy your work. To that end, you want to make sure you're writing and selling content that is worth its price. Without an introduction to tiers of quality, you might end up investing all of your time and energy into information products that you would then have to sell for a fraction of their worth. With a tiered marketing system, on the other hand, your purpose is more directed when you write.

In a nutshell, given the nature of the online marketplace and the ways in which consumers use web pages, there are three general tiers of information products. The first tier, in this book referred to as "entry level", consists of information products that serve to orient readers to your products and services. This tier should also offer some value to the consumer, but not so much that the consumer decides he or she no longer needs your more appropriately priced information products. The best way to think about this tier is as an appetizer at a nice restaurant. Consumers should enjoy it, but they should be left ready for more substantial content once they've successfully consumed the material of this tier.

To that end, the information products of this tier are often designed with a call to action to sign up for the most comprehensive products and services that you have to offer. The best way to do this is to offer some significant value, and then briefly outline the additional value that the consumer might gain from your more advanced and higher priced information products. These days, some online business owners choose to sell their information products at a very low price or; alternatively, they choose to offer it for free on a time-limited basis. The purpose of this is to spread the name of the business to the general population of the niche and, perhaps more importantly, to forge a personal connection with the consumer. The purpose of the personal connection is to make the consumer feel understood, which in turn reinforces the personalized nature of the information product. The information product is personalized due to the hard work you put into creating the consumer avatar, as well as your qualitative inquiry into the niche culture itself.

Your entry level content should refer both to your second- and third-tier content. The second-tier content, called "core" content, is the regularly updated content that your customers will look forward to each week. The core content keeps them engaged. You might classify core content like a blog, updated newsletter, or other publication. Core content could also be a routine service.

The best way to profit from core content is to divide its purpose into two. Think of it as content that exists between the third-tier content and the first-tier content, and then split it in half. Some of your core content will be free, but your customers will need to visit your website on a regular basis in order access it, which in turn keeps them involved in the community you've created within the overall niche subculture. On the other hand, most of your core content should be set aside for a members' area or other kind of paid subscription. The purpose of this is to create a relatively passive stream of income. You may need to do some work every week to maintain your core information products and the interests of those who consume it.

Beyond how to sell the core content, there is another important concept that is specific to core content. The core content represents your brand to the outside world, and it informs the norms of the culture within your online business. Eventually, it should begin to sell itself as people become increasingly interested in it. Furthermore, the core content will eventually inform the third-tier content.

Third-tier content is referred to as "upsell" content because it should be sold for a higher price than the entry-level and core content. Upsell content refers to eBooks, magazines, and other exclusive services that you might offer. For example, if you are a life coach, upsell products might be an exclusive consultation with you about a specific matter that is in high demand in the niche to which you sell your products and services.

You may wish to upsell products from your personal website. However, depending on the nature and format of these exclusive information products, you can sell them on other venues, such as online marketplaces or even in physical locations. For example, if you wrote a book and it was published, you could sell this upsell product in a local bookstore and then promote it heavily through tier-one and tier-two information products.

Synergizing Your Product Tiers

Online businesses are particularly fun to create and manage because the Internet provides so much creative license, and as technology improves so does your capacity to integrate and synergize the advertising campaigns of your various product tiers. If you want to create a successful online business and make the most profit from a given niche, you have to integrate your advertisements in an appealing, elegant, and even possibly entertaining way.

Many websites use a strategy that has become increasingly popular because it is non-invasive, yet grabs the attention of potential customers every time. The basic model is to create an entry-level product, such as a free YouTube video or guest blog post, that increases traffic to the core content on your main web page. Once there, use WordPress functions, hire a web developer, or learn JavaScript to set a timed message to your visitors. The message will address the reason the visitor likely came to your website, and then it will promote an upsell product that offers something relevant to that reason. This strategy is proven to be effective, and users consistently report that they find it a helpful advertising strategy.

Maximizing information product sales are the key to success in online business. The concepts and tools you learned in this book can make or break your online business. They will be reviewed and elaborated upon later in this book, but for now, it is recommended that you go back once more and familiarize yourself with the content of this chapter. In fact, the content in this chapter could be enough on its own to get you started in creating and marketing high-quality informational content if you weren't a business owner. Put another way. This chapter contains what is perhaps the most valuable information about getting your high-quality content out to consumers, irrespective of issues such as profit or the success of business.

Chapter 6: Create An Information Product Starting With A Smartphone And A PC

Many people choose to start online businesses because the cost is quite low, especially if the business is mostly or purely information-based. Although you may choose to reach out to potential customers with a variety of media strategies in the future, it is best to take advantage of the low overhead costs available through the Internet. Depending on your skill-set and the skills of those in your immediate circle of colleagues, you could potentially create, operate, and grow a successful online business for as little as a few dollars per year. In this chapter, you'll learn about a variety of information products you can create in the comfort of your home and share with potential customers right away.

Podcasts And Other Audio Recordings

Do you offer a self-help service, such as guided hypnosis, guided imagery, or meditation instructions? Are you a writer interested in making your products available to those who prefer not to read? Perhaps you're a popular speaker and hate to write? If you answered "yes" to any of these questions, you might want to consider making an audio recording for your customers.

These days, most computers and smartphones have built-in microphones, and the recording quality is quite good. Simply write up a script, or improvise, and record. There are some free audio editing programs available on the web for you to download and use to enhance the quality of your audio recordings or otherwise edit to perfection.

The best part, though, is that the Internet makes it incredibly easy to market and sell audio recordings via some online platforms. Or, if you like, you can use your audio recordings as free "core" information products.

eBooks

Depending on your niche, eBooks can function as an incredibly successful information product. One common yet effective strategy among internet marketers these days is to encourage people to offer visitors a free informational eBook as thanks for visiting their site and consuming their core content. In addition to the core content, the free informational eBook should add some value to your customer's lives. In return, you ask and encourage your customers to sign up for your mailing list and to consider purchasing some of your upsell products down the road. This strategy is particularly effective for gathering and retaining a high-volume client list, and those clients will return for your business because they feel that you value their satisfaction.

As with audio informational products, the Internet has made writing and publishing eBooks accessible to everyone. Gone are the days of negotiating with publishing houses and hiring expensive editors and proofreaders. As long as you know your stuff, and you're prepared to do the work to create a high-quality eBook, you can write it and publish it yourself. Smashwords is a very popular online independent publisher that allows you to publish virtually any eBook and sell it both on your website and on larger online marketplaces such as Amazon and Barnes & Noble.

Newsletters And Blog Posts

Newsletters might seem like an outdated information product, but depending on your niche, they can be highly effective. Do you run a job/event board, or other high-traffic website featuring frequent updates? A quality newsletter is both rare and highly desirable these days. If you've got the patience to put one together on a regular basis, your newsletter will be an excellent way to reach potential customers and maintain your customers' interest for years to come. With a newsletter, you'll likely get regular lifelong supporters of your business.

One extra feature of the newsletter, however, is its accessibility. As smart phones become increasingly sophisticated, many people pull up newsletters and articles throughout the day. In major cities, professionals are constantly glued to their tablets and smart phones. Just think: They could be reading your newsletter!

Alternatively and, depending on your niche, perhaps more realistically, those commuters could be reading your blog. Did you know that some bloggers earn a six-figure income? A high-quality blog will attract regular readers who will come to trust your expertise or rely on your wit and humor.

But blogs have an extra advantage. A good blog chronicles some growth and change. The growth and change might be in the maturity and sophistication of your writing, or perhaps the blog could chronicle the various countries you've traveled to or the aging of your pets. No matter the content, this natural tendency of blogs to chronicle growth and change makes it easy to convert the content of your blog into an eBook, which you can then market as an upsell product.

Vlogs

Video blogs, also known as "Vlogs," are another great way to reach a wide audience and retain repeat customers for years to come. As with audio recording technology, most computers, and smart phones have high-quality video recording technology already installed, so you can get to work creating your first Vlog with nothing more than a script and your usual computing technology.

One of the great things about Vlogs is that they go viral pretty quickly if the content is of high quality. Video sites such as YouTube are incredibly helpful for building a large clientele and establishing yourself and your brand as an expert in your niche. Furthermore, social video sites allow users to rate and comment, thus adding another dimension of consumer investment in your product and brand. Finally, these sites are great places to sell advertising space, which can, in turn, create a steady, reliable, and substantial stream of passive income.

Mobile Apps

Another great way to reach potential customers is by creating a mobile app. Although most apps are quite sophisticated, some home study might be all you need to get started making your very own mobile apps today! The best thing about mobile apps is that they are easily accessible and, depending on the design and usability, your customers will enjoy accessing your app in a variety of settings throughout the day. If you've got the funds, you might consider hiring an app developer to assist you.

Although mobile apps are not traditionally considered to be information products, they can be if they promote your core content in some way. For example, if you have an online business that aims to assist people in eating more nutritious food, you might design an app that includes a feature reminding people to check in at the website for various updates or recipes.

Information products might seem simple, but they are highly effective solutions sought by people who want to solve a problem or otherwise bring value to their lives. Think about it this way. An information product is something that might be very simple for you to create, but that might immensely benefit the lives of people who have trouble with what comes naturally to you. An information product is analogous, perhaps, to sitting down with an expert as a layperson and interviewing him or her about a specific problem you are having that could be solved by their expertise. In this sense, you can justify giving away information products if they bring customers back to your paid and upsell products. These concepts will be elaborated upon in later chapters of this book, but it's important to be thinking about them now, as this is a pivotal moment in your maturity as an online business founder, owner, and operator.

Chapter 7: How To Register A Domain Name

There is a folk legend about the famous sculptor, Michelangelo. The story goes that didn't draft plans or mark his stones before sculpting, as did his contemporaries. Rather, he was known to sit simply and stare at the stone for days on end before setting to work, at which point he would produce a beautiful artwork deftly and with ease. Although this is not a viable strategy for creating a business and designing a website, it is an effective learning model and, to that end, describes how this book is designed. So far, you've been guided through a series of exercises, instructions, and concepts in an order intended to get you thinking about the kind of business you'd like to create, who you'd like to market your products to, and the kinds of products you'd like to offer. All of this information was shared with the assumption that you'd be creating and running an online business. In our analogy here, think of the website as the block of stone.

In this chapter, you'll be introduced to the simple step of registering your domain name. Once you've completed this task, you'll be ready to set to work creating your website, uploading content, reaching out to possible customers, and optimizing it for search engines. All of those steps will be available to you in the following chapters. Without further ado, the following steps will guide you through the process of selecting and registering your domain name.

Step 1: Select A Domain Name

This step can be simple, or it can be complex depending on your aspirations and the nature of your business. This book stresses the importance of taking advantage of the Internet's various opportunities to simplify your work load so that you can devote the bulk of your time to creating high-quality content for your customers. To that end, simply choose a domain name that represents your business.

Wondering what a domain name is? A domain name is anything followed by ".com" or ".org" or some other similar variation. For example, "google.com" is a domain name. Beyond that, think of a domain name as analogous to the name of a small business. A domain name is essentially what your customers type into the search bar, and therefore think about, to reach your business web page.

If you're stumped, remember these rules of thumb:

1. Keep it simple.

2. One or two words is ideal.

3. Keep it straightforward.

4. Be direct.

5. When in doubt, abbreviate.

6. Keep it relevant.

Step 2: Register Your Domain Name

To register a domain name, simply head over to GoDaddy, HostGator, BlueHost, or another popular and reputable domain name vendor and apply for the rights to your desired domain name. Typically, domain names are good for about a year and cost between five and thirty dollars depending on the web host. Some companies, such as WordPress, offer both web hosting and free web design tools. These may be convenient and viable options depending on the nature of your business.

In preparation for the next chapter, you may want to select the option to include WordPress installation in the purchase of your domain name. Most reputable web hosts offer this option as WordPress is a very popular tool for web design. Although there are other ways for beginners to build websites, this book endorses WordPress as the ideal way for beginners to create their first online business website.

And there you have it: Your domain name is born! The next step will be to create your website. If the domain name is the title of your business, the website is the face of your business. This is a pivotal moment in the creation of your online business, as you transition from conceptual matters to the real-life launch of your new enterprise. Congratulations!

Chapter 8: Build Your Website, Even Without Any Skills

Although web design is an incredibly valuable service for any business owner, there are some ways to create a high-quality website on your own without any prior experience. The best resource for beginners is WordPress. As mentioned in the previous chapter, WordPress offers both web design tools and web hosting services. However, you can use the web design tools even if you use another web host, such as GoDaddy, for example. As WordPress and similar design sites are the easiest and most highly recommended tools for beginners with no prior experience in web design, the rest of this chapter will focus on how to access these templates, followed by user experience concepts necessary to create a web page that your customers will love to visit.

Creating A Website

Step 1: Getting Started With WordPress

Go ahead and either open up the WordPress design tools you downloaded and installed when creating your domain name or download and install WordPress from the official website. Once open, take some time to familiarize yourself with the tools and other options available to you. The great thing about WordPress is that everything is very easy to change and edit, so you don't have to worry about ruining anything.

Step 2: Consider The Purpose Of Your New Internet Home

Are you building a website, blog, or both? If you don't know the answer right away, it might be helpful to think about it this way. A website is a great way to showcase your products. On your website, you might direct users to a forum, your online store, or vendors that sell your products, such as eBooks, audio recordings, and so on. You might also use a website to gather customer contact information, and then send a regular newsletter to maintain ongoing contact. Finally, a website is an ideal choice if you plan to sell goods or services directly, as you can add options to sell and buy, including PayPal plugins through WordPress.

In contrast to a website, which is largely used to showcase your projects, a blog is ideal if you want the domain to be the product itself. Blogs can still be used to direct your customers to products and services, but they are most effectively used to provide regular content updates. Even though you might not sell products and services directly through your blog, blogging can be a highly lucrative occupation. As a blogger, you become a brand, a known and respected authority in your chosen niche, and your blog in turn becomes a valuable hub for advertisers and others who might wish to hire you for your expertise.

Perhaps your business model emphasizes both regular blog updates and plenty of goods and services to sell to your patrons. The best model, in that case, is to build a combined website and blog. Bigger is better, but when it comes to website design, you want to make sure all of your content is used appropriately, and you want to trim excess so that your loyal customers don't end up getting bored with your brand. To that end, although you might be tempted to make both the blog and the website, only do this if you truly have enough high-quality content to justify doing both.

Step 3: Consider Your Landing Page

The landing page is the first thing your visitors will see when they visit your website, so you want to make sure it's designed well. The main thing when it comes to the landing page is simplicity combined with ease of access to quality content. One common design for the landing page is to include a menu bar with options at the top, a company logo or name in the center, and an appropriate image or soft color in the background. Experiment with the design tools in WordPress to find out what works best given the nature of your business and the services you offer.

Step 4: Create An About Me Page

As a business owner, you want to be easily accessible to potential customers and clients. That's why it's important to create an "about me" page. If the landing page is the face of your business, the "about me" page is the persona that you, as the creator of the business, show to the world. In your "about me" page, list your interests, the kind of value you hope to offer to your patrons, and your inspiration for creating the business. Keep it simple and relatable.

Step 5: Create A Contact Us Page

You want to make sure your customers can get in touch with your business. Likely, this will be you, but you want to create a generic "contact us" page so that customers can get in touch with any administrative staff you may choose to hire down the road as your business begins to generate more income. The best "contact us" pages have a form for visitors to enter their personal and contact information, and then to submit a question or query.

Have you ever sent an email to a business and received a pleasant automatic response that was tailored to the query you submitted? There's a good chance that email was generated by autoresponder software. As a business owner, you'll want to get your hands on autoresponder software and put it to good use.

Consistent with the general theme of this book, you'll likely want to use the autoresponder plugin that comes with WordPress. It's an excellent tool, designed with meticulous attention to the needs of businesses, and best of all, it is available to you at no cost.

Step 6: Launch Your Page And Experience It For Yourself

After you've done all of the above and added your pages as you see fit and after you've developed a coherent and consistent design for your page, your final step is to go through and see how it feels from a customer's perspective. So, log on and test-drive your site. Make sure all of the information is easily accessible and that the overall layout is intuitive and easily mastered. Make sure it's aesthetically pleasing, too.

There you have it! Your website is built. Now it's time to set up systems that will help you generate traffic, retain customers, and build the income generated by your business.

Chapter 9: Create A Mail Funnel That Sells

Mail funnels are the bread and butter of any online business. A quality mail funnel allows you to reach out to prospective customers, offer them some valuable information, and keep them coming back for more. Gradually, with a quality mail funnel, you'll find that you have customers consuming a variety of product tiers and your upsell sales will be increasing rapidly.

Before getting into the finer points of creating a mail funnel that sells, it's important to understand what exactly qualifies a mail funnel. A mail funnel is a process by which clients are drawn into your business, offered an incentive to stay connected with the happenings of the business, and then progressively invited to purchase increasingly higher-priced products. There are simple and complex mail funnels, and the one you choose to implement will depend on the overall structure of your business.

If you offer one basic class of products, or a range of "one size fits all" products, you should stick with a simple mail funnel. This kind of mail funnel will consist of cold calls and cold emails to people who might populate your niche followed by tiered advertisements ultimately leading to your upsell products.

On the other hand, if you offer a variety of products that might appeal to a diverse range of customers, you'll want to go with a more complex mail funnel. These mail funnels will need to be monitored and operated manually to some extent, but it's worth it as you have the potential to generate multiple streams of high income. With a complex mail funnel, you will have the ability to reach out to a general population and then guide them through different funnels depending on select variables such as age, location, and interests.

Although complex mail funnels are interesting and fun to set up and operate, this book will focus on the simple mail funnel. The reason for this is you need to learn the simple mail funnel before you can successfully construct a more complicated one. However, once you've got the simple mail funnel down, constructing a complicated mail funnel is a breeze, and the only "complicated" part becomes manually operating them.

Without further ado, here are the steps to create a mail funnel that sells.

Step 1: Think Like A Marketer

Running your own online business allows you an unprecedented amount of freedom, but with freedom comes responsibility. As an online business owner, you will likely be responsible for many, if not all, of the responsibilities that would ordinarily be allocated to various specialists. Primarily, however, as an online business owner, you will need to both offer high-quality products and market those products to prospective customers.

At this point, it is assumed that you've more or less got the creation of quality products down. If not, you might consider returning to some of the earlier parts of this book before moving forward. The reason for this is, even the best marketer will be unsuccessful if the product is not good. The preliminary step to running a successful email funnel campaign, then, is to ensure that you have quality products to offer to your valued customers.

If you do have quality products that you firmly believe will contribute value to your customers, you can begin to think of your mail funnel as a tool to get that product out to as many people who might benefit from your product as possible. This line of thinking is important to internalize, because without it one is liable to fall into the dark side of marketing, in which case your business is likely to become entirely profit driven and, as a result, you are liable to suffer burnout because you are no longer doing what you love, which was the entire purpose of starting an online business in the first place.

Now, with these preliminary tasks and organizing concepts taken care of, you're ready to begin thinking like a marketer. The first step to running a successful mail funnel is to be constantly thinking about just how exactly it is that your products and services will add value to the lives of others. From there, you need to consider the possibility that everyone you interact with is a potential lead. When wearing your "marketing hat", so to speak, you will then always be prepared to either guide those potential leads through processes that might bring them closer to increasingly expensive products which, in turn, will add more and more value to their lives. Or, if those potential leads are unprepared to purchase your products at this time, you, as a marketing guru, will have invited them into the community that exists around your products, and in doing so you will have accessed their friends, families, and acquaintances, who in turn will be potential leads themselves.

The basic process you will guide people through is: 1) Those interested in your business and its products (Leads); 2) Those aware of, and/or passively involved in the community aspect of your business and its products (Prospects); and 3) Those actively involved in the culture of your business and frequently consuming its products. The mail funnel will be your primary tool in guiding people through these three stages.

Step 2: Generate Leads

Just to recap, leads are people who either have no information about your business or who only know of it superficially. When it comes to leads, you are mostly interested in how to reach them, then how to convert them to prospects. In other words, you want to find people who don't know about your business and its products, and then educate them about those matters.

For many online business owners, this can feel like the most daunting task. However, with these simple tips, it can be relatively simple and painless. There are many ways to generate leads. The first and most basic are to produce free content on a regular basis that will add value to people's lives. These can be videos on YouTube, regular blog posts, or anything else. The main idea is that it is simple, doesn't take you very much time to do, yet adds some value to the lives of those who consume this product, such that they come back for more.

Another strategy is to place ads in the newspaper, on media sites, or even around town. You can create business cards or flyers and distribute them in local cafes, for example. This strategy is often adopted by larger companies with more money to put into advertising, but you can do it with a small business if you advertise strategically and keep the materials simple. The only trick here is to make sure your advertising materials are tasteful. Poor advertising could drive potential customers away from your business, and this is especially popular when you're not using the Internet.

Another very successful way to generate leads is to use social media. For this reason, social media is an essential part of any online business owner's repertoire. With social media, you can reach thousands of people across the globe and keep them engaged in what you're doing. You can also use social media to network with colleagues and major players in your particular niches. Another great thing about social media is that it allows you to gauge how many people might be actively involved in your business through subscriber counts. Finally, with social media, you can develop an active presence in niche-specific online communities. For example, with Twitter and Facebook, you can connect with the major players in a niche community and further get your name out to those potential leads.

To that end, and this is the last strategy for generating leads, you should be actively involved in as many niche-specific communities as you have time for. This means going to events and networking there. It means building a social circle on social media platforms. It means putting your name out there in strategic ways.

All of this should be in the service of getting people to visit your landing page, which was discussed earlier in this book. Briefly, to recap, the purpose of the landing page is to convert your leads to prospects. This is where your autoresponder technology comes in. Carry on to the next step to learn more about this pivotal step in lead conversion through mail funnels.

Step 3: Convert Leads To Prospects And Convert Prospects To Customers

As with leads, it is important to recall briefly what prospects are before moving forward. Prospects are, in a nutshell, people who have expressed some interest in your business by, in the case of Internet businesses, visiting your landing page. Your goal is to convert prospects into customers. As mentioned in the preceding section, your autoresponder comes in handy here.

Essentially, you want to set up your landing page such that customers are greeted with a sales pitch. However, you don't necessarily want your customer to think of it as a "sales pitch" per se. Rather, you want to communicate to your customer that, although you make your living through your business, you are first and foremost dedicated to the happiness and wellbeing of your customers. To that end, you might include a video pitch of the above sentiment, or you might communicate this through writing. Better yet, you've already communicated this when generating leads and, to that end, have remained consistent and congruent with the sentiment throughout the entire process.

Now is the time to see if you can ask your customer to consider getting more involved in your business community and, possibly down the road, purchasing some of your products and services. The difficulty here is that if you are too aggressive in your marketing, you risk driving your customers away, so you want to emphasize that your number one priority is to improve their lives. You want to pump the benefits.

Somewhere on your landing page, you should give your leads, who have now become your prospects by having visited your landing page, an incentive to stay in contact with you. The best way to do this is to ask your prospects for their email addresses and to tell them that in return you will send them more of the valuable products you've designed. You can do this by creating a product, an eBook perhaps, and offer to send it to them free of charge if they sign up for an email list from you.

Once you've got your prospect's email address, it's time to include them in the mail funnel. The best way to do this is to set up your autoresponder to thank your prospects for signing up, to include the eBook, and to edit the settings to direct them to other products and services if they reply to any of your emails. Otherwise, think about the mail funnel as a series of emails that will guide prospects to different products and services.

As stated before, the first email is simply introductory and thank you letter. A second email should go out a few days later that checks in on how the prospects are enjoying whatever free product you've offered them. In the case of our example, this product would be an eBook. In this second email, you can also ask your prospects if they have any feedback for you, and you can remind them to visit your website, which in turn will bring them back to all of the wonderful products you have to offer them.

From there, you can send more emails spaced out at particular intervals. These emails should function to get people to keep coming back to your website, to get involved with your brand, and ultimately to receive value from your work on a regular basis. In your additional emails, you can begin to introduce people to your upsell products. You might make exclusive email offers also.

Step 4: Retain Customers

Once people start buying into your brand, they can be considered customers. From there, the challenge is to get your customers to stay, possibly for a lifetime and benefit from all of the great products you have to offer. One surefire way to find and retain customers is to initiate what is called a "call to action" in your email funnel.

The call to action is essentially some incentive for people to participate in your brand. Strategies might be as simple as encouraging people to comment on your videos or blog posts. Another is to encourage people to buy products that they might find particularly beneficial to their personal lives, and then to comment on how the products have helped them.

Another strategy is to introduce complicated email funnels that are catered to your preferred customer's needs. These customers will appreciate the individual attention, and will, in turn, recommend your services to others. This is how word spreads and businesses go viral. When customers reach out, you suddenly have multiple people generating leads, and your lead-base, followed by your prospect base, followed by your customer base grows exponentially.

You'll also need a way for customers to reach you or a customer support specialist easily. Your autoresponder technology will come in handy once again here. In addition to a pleasant array of autoresponses, you'll want to list your business email or a customer support email, and you'll want to be sure to respond to these preferred and repeat customers promptly and sensitively. This, in turn, will generate more responses to your calls to action, and those responses will be increasingly positive, which will in turn raise the positivity of your overall business community.

Chapter 10: Clickbank: How To Boost Your Sales With No Effort

Clickbank is an excellent tool to boost your online sales with virtually no effort. You can earn money in a variety of ways using Clickbank. In this chapter, we'll give you an overview of those methods, and then you can choose the methods that seem best to you.

The first method is perhaps the most popular. Do you ever review products on your business website? If so, you can purchase affiliate links from Clickbank and post them throughout your website. Alternatively, if you are well established in a niche, you can purchase affiliate links from your business contacts and promote those businesses. In turn, you will earn a small percentage of their sales.

One of the great things about Clickbank is that you can use it to promote not only your own business but also businesses and products that you feel will benefit the lives of your valued customers. It is an excellent way not only to make money but also to build and strengthen professional relationships. With Clickbank, you can build many passive income streams, which you can then use to fuel your business.

If you run a popular blog, Clickbank should be your go-to for generating income and adding value to your customer's lives by promoting products that they will enjoy. You could even potentially build a reputable online business solely by promoting high-quality products in a personalized fashion.

With Clickbank, you can also promote your products. You can register your products and services with Clickbank, and then pay others to advertise for you. In that sense, you not only give something back to all of the members of your niche community, which in turn generates soft leads but you also actively generate hard leads by reaching out to other Internet marketers. With Clickbank, you can grow your leads and prospects exponentially, often in a passive way.

The best part is that Clickbank is very simple to use. If you're promoting other people's accounts, simply register and sign up for affiliate links. Once you have them, embed them in your informational products. On the other hand, if you're promoting your products, simply create affiliate links and offer them to prospective Internet marketers.

Although Clickbank is a relatively straightforward tool to use, there is one strategy that is often overlooked, yet that can earn you thousands of dollars if applied correctly. That tool is called "cloaking." You want to "cloak" or disguise your affiliate links in a particular way. Here is what I mean: When you sign on for a particular affiliate link, you get the URL.

However, Internet surfers are reluctant to click on links that are blatant advertisements. Think about it; we're bombarded with advertisements all the time. Why would anyone in their right mind leave perfectly valuable content to look at an advertisement?

So the trick is to "cloak" the URL in regular text. The easiest way to do this is with WordPress tools or basic HTML. You simply choose some text to stand in for the link. One of the classic strategies is to write an extensive review of a product or a blog post in which the product is casually named. In the latter example, you might consider writing a blog post that addresses a particular problem or concern, and then casually list some products for which you have affiliate links. The best and easiest way to casually mention a product is to name drop simply and then write some text that says something like, "*You can find said product by clicking here.*"

That quoted text would be the "cloaked" link, in this case. When visitors click on it, they will be taken to the product page and, in turn, you will be paid for your services. Some people raise ethical concerns about the practice of cloaking affiliate links, but if you think about it, you're not doing anything wrong if you truly believe the products you direct customers to will add value to their lives. In fact, if you think about it that way, you're doing them a service when you bypass their initial gut reaction to screen out your advertisement as they do with most other advertisements. When you cloak an ad that you truly believe in, you give customers the opportunity to discover a product or service they might ordinarily not have ever known about.

Conclusion

Thank you again for downloading this book!

I hope this book was able to help you to create your very own online business from scratch.

The next step is to get started in your online business adventure. With the tools you've learned in this book, you will be able to live your dreams as you create and manage an online business built around your biggest passion. The best part is that you already know many of the basic principles, and with this book now you have the skills. I wish you the very best in your business ventures. May you bring massive value to the lives of others, and may you profit from your generosity.

Finally, if you enjoyed this book, please take the time to share your thoughts and post a review on Amazon. It'd be greatly appreciated!

Thank you and good luck!

www.ingramcontent.com/pod-product-compliance
Lightning Source LLC
Chambersburg PA
CBHW070420190526
45169CB00003B/1344